WHAT ALL STOCK AND MUTUAL FUND INVESTORS SHOULD KNOW!

By Bruce Sankin

D1519084

Copyright 1990, 1992, 2003, 2004 by Bruce Sankin,

Revised 2002, 2003, 2004, 2005, 2008, 2009,2010-2012

Published by: Bruce N. Sankin

PO Box 77-1502, Coral Springs. Florida 33077

TABLE OF CONTENTS

About the Author

Bruce Sankin is a former stockbroker, having worked for Prudential-Bache & Dean Witter. He has a Bachelor of Science degree in finance and was a member of the Law Society. Mr. Sankin writes a column on arbitration and has been interviewed in many publications like Money Magazine and The Wall Street Journal. He has appeared on national television and has been used for his expert opinion in arbitration cases. He is also an arbitrator specializing in securities.

He currently is based in Coral Springs, Florida.

Know Your Rights as a 401k Investor

By Bruce Sankin, National Consumer Advocate on Investors Rights

If you are a participant in a 401k plan, it also means you are an investor. As an investor, you MUST become educated about your financial future! I am a financial author and columnist; in addition, I am a consumer advocate for investor's rights. It always amazes me how people who have 401k plans really do not take an interest in knowing their rights when it comes to their financial future.

Here is an example: If you go to a mall and buy a television, or clothes, or any other product and realize there is a problem with the product, you know exactly what your rights are and instinctively know what to do. You go back to the store with your receipt, tell the salesperson there is a problem, and ask for a refund. If the salesman says no you ask for the manager. If the manager says no you go all the way up the line until you get your money back. Yet, when it comes to your investments in your 401k plan, which could be tens of thousands if not hundreds of thousands of dollars, if there is a problem, most people do not know their rights or what to do. You MUST become an aggressive consumer with your investments the same way you are with other products and services!

Remember, after your physical health, your financial health is paramount!

What do I mean by being an aggressive consumer?

1. Know all fees, performance data, and investment objectives before investing.
2. Read prospectus before investing.
3. Understand asset allocation and invest accordingly.
4. Know exactly who to contact when you have questions about your 401k.
5. If your investment objectives, or life situation changes (you get married. divorced, widowed, change jobs, etc.) review and alter investments to ensure they reflect new realities.

Be smart. Be wise. And be aggressive!

Plan administrators should also be communicating to their plan participants that since they own mutual funds, they need to become an educated, informed investor who knows their rights as an investor. Help arm them with the right questions.

Bruce Sankin, a consumer advocate and columnist, is the author of "What All Stock and Mutual Fund Investors Should Know!" The manual, which is used by state regulatory agencies, Division of Securities, and plan sponsors as an educational tool designed to enhance investor literacy.

CHAPTER ONE
HOW TO SAVE MONEY
ON BUYING AND SELLING STOCKS

A financial advisor receives a commission for the service of buying or selling your stock. If you want to know your commission cost before deciding to make a trade, just call your advisor and he will be able to give it to you. It should be noted that your advisor has the authority to offer you a 5%-20% discount. However, most advisors will not volunteer this information. In today's world of the Internet and online trading, always ask for the discount.

It is not in the advisor's best interest to give you a large discount because some brokerage firms pay less of a commission to the advisor if the discount exceeds a certain percentage. Financial advisors work on what is called a "grid." The percentage of commission an advisor receives is dependent upon the amount of business the broker generates for the brokerage firm. For example, if the advisor is on a 35% payout grid, he is entitled to 35% of the commission that the brokerage firm charges you. If, however, the advisor discounts a stock trade more than his firm permits, they may pay him less than 35% of the commissions.

Remember, **BROKERAGE FIRMS WILL ALLOW LARGER DISCOUNTS**. Sometimes the advisor will need the office manager's approval. Ask your advisor to ask their manager for a larger discount. Many managers may not want you to know that the firm can offer a larger discount because managers receive a percentage of the total revenue the office generates, so larger discounts will mean less money for him.

If you want to buy 200 shares of stock at a price of $20.00 per share, the total cost would be $4,000.00 plus your commission. At a full service brokerage firm, the commission rate could be as much as 3.1% of the purchase price of the stock, or $125, in the above example. This is very expensive. Usually a fair price is considered to be between 1% and 2%. Thus, you can, and should negotiate with your advisor.

An alternative to negotiating your commission is to tell your advisor that you want to trade on a per share basis. Trading on a per share basis is when you pay a flat amount on each share of stock that you trade as opposed to a percentage of the total purchase price of that stock. It is possible to negotiate a $0.05 to $0.10 per share cost with your broker. **Tell your advisor what you are willing to pay him.** Some online companies will charge a flat $10.00 commission for a thousand share trade. If your advisor tells you he will not do the trade at the commission cost you want, then find a company that will. There will always be financial advisors who are looking for business.

If you are directing the transactions in your account, i.e. telling your broker what to buy or sell, then his services are of limited value to you anyway since he is merely an order taker. You should have a say in deciding how much money his services are worth.

You must not forget that a financial advisor is a commissioned salesman; he wants and needs your business. Do not believe them if they says they do not want your business. **That is how they make their living.** He does not want to lose your business, or for you to get advice from anyone else. If your advisor really does not want to do your trade at your price, do not worry, you will always find a financial advisor who will, you just need to look.

CHAPTER TWO
BONDS

If you ask, your advisor has to tell you their commission on a purchase or sale of a stock. Likewise, if you ask, they have to tell you the sales charge when you purchase or sell a mutual fund. However, when you want to buy a bond, whether it is a tax free municipal bond, most corporate bonds, or a treasury bond, your advisor does not have to tell what he and the firm are making on the transaction. This is because bonds are bought and sold on a mark-up or mark-down basis and mark-ups or mark-downs do not have to be disclosed. Buying or selling a bond with a mark-up and mark-downs rather than commissions is called buying or selling 'net".

If you go to your advisor to buy a tax free municipal bond and he says the price is $10,000.00 net, he will generally tell you that the price includes commissions. You can still find out what the cost to you of the transaction is by asking the advisor what the firm would pay you if you wanted to sell the same bond to them. If, for example, the answer was that the firm would pay you $9,600.00 if they were buying it from you, then the actual cost (spread) of the bond is $400.00 or 4%.

If you ask your advisor what the buying or selling price of a bond is, this price is usually on his computer. He can also wire or email his bond department to get the information. He also has other options. He can check his bond inventory on his computer. Brokerage firms keep an inventory of bonds to offer and sell to their clients. The potential problem is that bond prices could change daily. This means that the price of a specific bond could be different at different brokerage firms. Each brokerage firm charges a price they feel they can get for the bond. The difference between the bid and ask (sell and buy) given to the advisor by the bond department is generally 1/4 to 1% spread. This spread is what the bond department makes on the bond. Then the advisor adds on his commission which will usually be between 1/8% and 2%. **What you, as the client, are probably unaware of is that the broker may mark up or mark down the bond, depending on what he thinks you will pay for it or sell it for.** On a buy and sell of the same bond, the advisor and the brokerage firm together could make as much as 3% -4% on the trade.

At some full service firms, it is possible that you can negotiate bond prices. When he gives you a price for a bond you can usually negotiate between 1/4% and 1% of the price of the bond. On a $25,000.00 purchase or sale, you could save as much as $250.00. If your advisor does not want to give you this discount, then call other advisors and tell them what you are looking for. With billions of dollars of bonds for sale every day, there will be an advisor who can usually get your bond at your price. On the other hand, if your broker offers you a bond and, after calling other brokerage firms, you find it to be the best price, quote, and yield — **BUY IT.** Getting what you want is more important than knowing what the brokerage firm makes.

UNIT TRUSTS

In some instances brokerage firms or independent companies put a group of bonds together and sell them as a package. These packages are usually called "unit trusts". A unit trust may be preferable to individual bonds because it diversifies the risk among a group of bonds instead of putting all the money into one bond. Another benefit of the unit trust is that interest payments are made monthly as compared to an individual bond, where interest payments are made semi-annually. On the other hand, the cost of buying a unit trust is not cheap; it can range from 4% to 5% and is an integral part of the structure of the trust. Therefore, commissions on unit trusts cannot generally be negotiated.

The purchase of unit trusts is, however, subject to commission discounts in the form of "break points". This means that for certain volume purchases the commission will decrease. Common breakpoints in the purchase of unit trusts are $50,000, $100,000, and $250,000.00. Under a $100,000 purchase you may pay 4%% commission while at $100,000 you may pay 3 1/4%, at $250,000 2 1/2% etc. (It should be noted that your advisor receives a commission when you buy a unit trust. though not usually when you sell it.)

When you ask about a unit trust, your advisor will give you three quotations. He will quote you the price that you will pay if you want to buy it (ask price); the price that you will get if you want to sell it (bid price); and the actual value (par value) of the bonds in each unit of the trust. The par value is also the amount of money you will get back if you hold each unit to maturity (or to the call date, if the unit is priced to call.

When your advisor gives you a price and yield on a unit trust make sure he tells you two yields: the current yield and the yield to maturity or to call date. It is also important to find out if the bond in the unit trust has a call feature. This means that the company or municipality can buy the bonds back from the unit trust before maturity. It has no option if the bond gets called. The unit trust must sell it back; Make sure your advisor tells you what the yield to call is. It could be a lot less than a yield to maturity or current yield and you do not want any surprises after you buy the unit trust,

Be very careful when your broker gives you a quotation for a current yield on a unit trust that seems higher than an individual bond. If this does occur, ask him for the bid price, the ask price and the par value. For example, if he tells you that you will get 7.75% current return on a unit trust and a comparable individual bond is only giving 7.0% current return, then there is a good chance you are paying a premium for each unit trust.

A premium is the difference between what you pay (ask price) and the actual value (par price). If the ask price for the unit is $1,000.00 per unit and the par price is $900.00 per unit, you are paying $100.00 per unit or 10% more than the actual value. If you bought 10 units at $1,000.00 each and paid $10,000.00 and you held the units to maturity, you would only get back $9,000.00. You would get more interest income on your units each year, but in the end you would get less principal back then you put in. Premium bonds and unit trusts can be a good investment as long as you understand what you are giving up in principal for the extra yearly income. When buying bonds you should ask your advisor about the rating of the bonds or unit trusts. A rating will give you the quality and risk of each bond. The higher the quality, the less the risk, the lower the yield or "return on your investment". Conversely, the lower the quality, the higher the risk, and the higher the yield. Most bonds are rated by two rating companies: Standard & Poors, commonly known as S&P, and Moody's Investor Service.

The following is Standard & Poor's definition on rating of bonds:

AAA - Debt rated 'AAA' has the highest rating assigned by Standard & Poor's. Capacity to pay interest and repay principal is extremely strong.

AA- Debt rated 'AA' has a very strong capacity to pay interest and repay principal and differs from the higher rated issues only in small degree.

A Debt rated 'A' has a strong capacity to pay interest and repay principal although it is somewhat more susceptible to the adverse effects of changes in circumstances and economic conditions than debt in higher rated categories.

BBB- Debt rated 'BBB' is regarded as having an adequate capacity to pay interest and repay principal. Whereas it normally exhibits adequate protection parameters, adverse economic conditions or changing circumstances are more likely to lead to a weak ened capacity to pay interest and repay principal for debt in this category than in higher rated categories.

BB, B, CCC, CC, C -

Debt rated 'BB', 'B', `CCC', `CC' and 'C' is regarded, on balance, as predominantly speculative with respect to capacity to pay interest and repay principal in accordance with the terms of the obligation. `BB' indicates the lowest degree of speculation and 'C the highest degree of speculation. While such debt will likely have some quality and protective characteristics. these are out weighed by large uncertainties or major risk exposures to adverse conditions.

Bond Investment Quality Standards:

Under present commercial bank regulations issued by the Comptroller of the Currency, bonds rated in the top four categories (AAA', 'AA', 'A', 'BBB', commonly known as "Investment Grade" ratings) are generally regarded as eligible for bank investment. In addition, the Legal Investment Laws of various states may impose certain rating or other standards for obligations eligible for investment by savings banks, trust companies, insurance companies and fiduciaries generally.

There are also bonds known as nonrated or NR bonds. This means that for some reason S&P and/or Moody's have not rated the quality of that particular bond. It does not mean, however, that there is something wrong with the bond. If you are interested in a nonrated bond, ask your broker to find out the reason why it is not rated. If there is not a good reason why the bond has not been rated, then the best thing to do is to pass on that bond and find another bond with a rating that meets your satisfaction.

Many unit trusts are sold in a secondary market. This means that an individual sold the unit trust before maturity. Often, Unit Trusts sold before maturity are purchased by the brokerage firm and put into the brokerage firm's inventory. This means that you may be able to buy a unit trust that has a higher coupon, (premium) or lower coupon (discount) from the brokerage firm's inventory.

Individual bonds and unit trusts have something in common which buyers sometimes are unaware of. The face value of these investments is only paid at maturity. If you sold these investments before maturity, you would get the market value. Market value is the price the brokerage firm is willing to pay. This could be higher or lower than the amount you paid for it. Example: You bought a $10,000 General Electric bond that expires January 1, 2020. If you held the bond to maturity, General Electric would pay you $10,000 on January 1, 2020. If you sold this bond before January 1, 2020, it is strictly the brokerage firm's decision what price they will pay you for the bond.

CHAPTER THREE

MUTUAL FUNDS & ETFs

One of the largest types of investments today where financial advisors generate large commissions is mutual funds. Mutual funds are a simple way to invest in securities. You tell your advisor what you are looking for: stocks; bonds; an aggressive or conservative investment strategy; an income or an appreciation approach; then your advisor finds the mutual fund which fits your needs. Since advisors make commissions, they will usually sell you an open ended mutual fund that has a "load" or sales charge. Most stock funds with front end loads have sales charges between 4% and 7%. Bond funds have sales charges that range between 3% and 5%. Sales charges are usually reduced the more you invest. This is known as "break points" or, in simple terms, a volume discount.

In the early 1980's brokerage firms and mutual fund companies realized people did not like to pay an upfront sales charge, so they created a new type of sales charge called backend sales charge", or redemption fees". This means that you may pay a sales charge when you sell your shares back to the fund. Most backend load mutual funds have an additional annual expense to the shareholder known as the 12b-1 fee. This fee is used to promote and advertise the fund to other potential shareholders.

My opinion on mutual fund expenses is that annual fees are not as important as the fund's performance in both up markets and down markets. A mutual fund that does only 2% a year better then the S&P 500 will have 65% more value than the S&P index fund in twenty five years. This is known as the positive effect of "compounding".

If you want to buy a mutual fund but you don't want to use the services of a financial advisor you can always buy the fund yourself. If you are willing to put in the time, effort the hours of research to oversee your finances, you can buy no load mutual funds. There are many no load mutual funds with the same or similar types of securities and investment objectives that your advisor would purchase for you. If you have $10,000.00 to invest, one option would be to call up you broker and set up a meeting. At that meeting, you could discuss your financial needs. At the end of the meeting, after the broker did his due diligence he would probably recommend a specific mutual fund. If that mutual fund has a sales charge of 4% you have just paid him $400.00 for his professional financial advice. You now have to decide if your face to face meeting was worth it. Once the money goes into the mutual fund, performance is up to the portfolio manager.

IMPORTANT! - What is very important is that unless you know, and understand, how to select a no load mutual fund which meets your risk tolerance, investment objective, and suitability, you might be emotionally induced by the wrong factors to purchase a specific mutual fund. Unfortunately, many average and unsophisticated investors purchase a mutual fund based on its latest twelve-month performance without considering those other factors. Since we are talking about large amounts of money that could affect your financial future, unless you are willing to put in the time, effort, research, and monitoring of your money, the services of a qualified financial professional may be the better value.

If you decide to choose a mutual fund yourself, there are a number of sources you can use. Morningstar is a website that will give you the information you will need to make a fair judgment on thousands of mutual funds. Many financial advisors use this information in choosing mutual funds for their clients. Magazines like Money and Forbes publish special editions that describe and rate mutual funds. There are also newsletters that follow the mutual fund industry. Check Internet search engines for "Mutual Fund Newsletters' Monthly newsletters give recommendations and updates on most mutual funds,

If you don't want to put in the time and effort to find a no load fund and still want to use the services of a financial advisor to recommend a good family of funds, here is an idea on how to reduce the sales charge. Many excellent families of funds like M.F.S., Putnam, Delaware Group, American, Aim, etc. have different funds within the same family. All of these funds have exchange privileges, which means you can switch from one fund to another at net asset value. What your advisor might not be aware of is that different funds within the same family have different sales charges. This means you can buy a fund that has a load of 2 1/2%, and 30 days later you can exchange it for a fund you really wanted, which has a 5 3/4% load saving you 3 1/4% on the purchase of the fund. This could be hundreds of dollars or more in savings for you . These savings will range from 25%-60% of the sales charge. There are two types of mutual funds: open-end and closed-end. Open-end mutual funds consist of a portfolio of securities that trade at net asset value, or N.A.V. Net asset value is the total value of the securities in the fund at the end of each trading day divided by the number of shares outstanding of the fund. That is how you get the cost per share of an open-end mutual fund. Even if you buy an open-end mutual in the morning, your broker cannot tell you what you paid for the fund until the next day. Open-end also means the number of shares that can be purchased is unlimited. A closed-end fund is a fund which has a limited number of shares.

An open-end fund and a closed-end fund are similar in that they both have securities in their portfolio, they both charge shareholders for expenses, and they both have N.A.V.'s; however, unlike shares of an open-end fund, which is priced once at the end of the day at N.A.V, shares of a closed-end fund are traded freely in the open market. This means that shares could be bought and sold either below (a discount) or above (a premium) the fund's net asset value. Since the number of shares of a closed- end fund is limited; the price at which you either buy or sell your shares in the open market will depend on the demand for the shares. Clearly, then, there is an additional risk in a closed-end fund. Not only is there fluctuation in net asset value, but also in the demand for the shares, and because of this, there is also an opportunity. If you purchase shares of a closed-end fund whose shares are selling at a significant discount to the net asset value, it is possible in a rising market that not only will the net asset value increase, but the demand for the shares will also increase. This will narrow the discount and possibly put the share price at a premium to net asset value. You can find specific information on closed-end funds in the WALL STREET JOURNAL and BARRONS. They will have the share price, net asset value, and percentage of discount or premium so you can easily be fully informed.

Beginning in the mid 1990s a new type of mutual fund was created called an 'Exchange Traded Fund' or ETF. They are structured as a pool of stocks, bonds, or other assets. They are similar to closed end mutual funds in that they trade like a stock. They have a symbol and can be bought and sold on the open market all trading day. Since ETFs are traded like stocks, they have many advantages over open end mutual funds. You can put in a limit order, you can sell them short, you can buy options on many ETFs, and the commissions will be lower.

Why invest in mutual funds?

When I ask clients why they invest in mutual funds most of them laugh and say "like everyone else I want to make money". The answer is not as simple as 'I want to make money'. When I ask them to explain why they want their mutual funds to make money their answers differ from person to person. The one answer that was universal was they want to have enough money when they get older. Everyone realized that unless they are financially independent they will not be able to retire.

Most people do not understand that investing money is the same as working for a living. Here is what I mean. The definition of working is "an occupation in which you get paid a salary or commission" Well, money invested in mutual funds also gets paid. Depending on the type of mutual fund you invest in your money gets paid in three ways: interest income, dividends, or appreciation in value. **Financial independence means having your investments pay you as much as your occupation pays you.**
Only then will you be financially secure to retire. The problem is most people have no idea what they need to do today to have financial independence in twenty, thirty, or forty years. It amazes me when I speak to people and they tell me they planned a vacation and they know exactly how much money they will need. Yet when it comes to their retirement they have no idea how to figure it out.

I tell them that the same way they have a "Game Plan" for their vacation they need a "Game Plan" for their retirement. A game plan for your retirement is called a "Financial Analysis". Qualified financial professionals have the expertise and software to create a customized financial analysis. Based on the information you give them today they can project what you will need to retire. Remember, this is only a projection. The one thing that is guaranteed is that things change. I suggest you review your financial analysis with your financial professional every year. If your financial situation changes make sure it is updated. This is especially true if the bulk of your money is in an employer sponsored retirement plan. Make sure you contact the plan administrator annually. He will direct you to the financial professional who is there to educate you on your investments.

CHAPTER FOUR

ANNUITIES

When you are thinking about retirement, one of the first questions you ask yourself is 'how do I accumulate enough money to make sure I don't outlive my money?' Annuities are an option that may help you reach your retirement goal.

An annuity is simply a contract between you and an insurance company. You give the insurance company money and the insurance company guarantees that they will pay you a certain amount of money for a certain period of time. The amount of money the insurance company will pay you will be determined either at the time you buy the annuity or a date in the future. This will depend on the type of annuity you purchase.

The benefits of owning annuities as part of your financial planning for retirement is that any income, interest, or capital gains that the annuity earns or accumulates is tax deferred. This means you do not pay any taxes until you withdraw this money in the future. The ultimate goal is that you will not need to withdraw this money until you retire; when you should be in a lower tax bracket. Since annuities are funded with after tax dollars, when you begin to withdraw from the annuity, either immediately or in the future, a percentage of the money will be a return of your own money which is tax free. Only the interest or capital gains will be taxed.

Another benefit of an annuity is that you are required to name a beneficiary. At the time of your death your beneficiary will directly receive any benefits of the annuity. It will not go into your estate therefore bypassing probate. This benefit will save your heirs time and money. Another potential benefit of an annuity is it can be judgment proof in case of a legal dispute with creditors. This will depend on your state of residency and the length of time you own the annuity.

Annuities are similar to other investments you use for retirement. As an example, variable annuities use stock or bond mutual funds. Fixed annuities give you a fixed percentage on your investment for a fixed period of time, similar to a bank's Certificates of Deposit. In my opinion, a major benefit in buying an annuity is the guarantees and riders you can purchase with the annuity.

Insurance companies can offer you guarantees and riders. You have to decide if the cost is worth the benefit. Here is an example. You purchase two products for your retirement; an S&P 500 index fund and a fixed indexed annuity that has the S&P 500 index in the annuity. The index fund has annual expenses of under 1/2% per year. The fixed indexed annuity has no annual expense, but limits your gains. It guarantees that you will always get back a minimum of 100% of your investment, no matter how the stock market does; but may charge you a surrender charge over the life of the annuity.

Like any insurance product, the cost of the guarantee only matters if you need it. As long as the S&P 500 goes up, the pure index fund may be a better value because of the lower expenses. Your cost for the guarantee wasn't necessary.

In July, 2008, the US stock market was officially in a bear market. This means the market was down 20% from its November, 2007 high. The pure S&P 500 index fund was down 37% by the end of 2008 with no guarantee that it will ever get back to the original invested amount. The guarantee that was purchased with the fixed indexed annuity gave the investor 'peace of mind' knowing that no matter how much the S&P 500 index declines in value, at the end of 2008 he would have at least 100% of his investment, plus the guaranteed minimum return on the investment. You have to decide if the additional annual expense is worth your 'peace of mind'.

Many financial gurus say 'the past performance of equities has showed that equities have always appreciated in value over the 'long haul'. This statement is usually true. The problem is how long the 'long haul' is. If you bought a Nasdaq 100 index fund in March, 2000, nine years later, in 2009, you would still be down 50%. Will the Nasdaq 100 index ever get to its high of 5,000 again? Maybe, but you don't know how many more years it will take just to break even. An even better example is the Japanese stock market (Nikkei 225). In 1989 the Nikkei 225 index hit a high of 39,000. As of July, 2008, almost twenty years later, the Nikkei 225 is under 14,000. This represents a 65% loss over the past twenty years.

In my opinion, purchasing guarantees and riders that are offered with annuities are an important consideration when investing for your retirement.

There are three basic types of annuities: Fixed rate, Variable, and Fixed indexed annuity.

A fixed rate annuity will pay a fixed interest rate for a fixed period of time. An insurance company may offer an incentive or bonus rate for the first year and then guarantee a minimum rate for the remaining years.

Variable annuities may invest in stocks, bonds, or mutual funds. The rate of return on variable annuities will depend on the performance of each investment. In contrast with a fixed annuity, which will always guarantee your principal and the interest, there is no guarantee with a variable annuity on the return of your entire principal. Some insurance companies offer riders that will minimize your potential loss, or even guarantee your principal. Again, you have to decide if the cost is worth the benefit.

Fixed indexed annuities are a hybrid of both fixed and variable annuities. Insurance companies realized people want to participate in the potential growth in the stock market, but don't want the downside risk associated with the stock market. Fixed indexed annuities allow you to earn a percentage of the growth if the market goes up, but limits your downside risk. There are many different types of fixed indexed annuities with many different options, guarantees, and riders to choose from.

Each of these annuities has two options on how it will pay you. It will be either an immediate annuity or a deferred annuity. Each of these annuities has different investment objectives with many payout options. In my opinion, only after you do a professional financial analysis that will plan your retirement objectives can you decide which type of annuity will meet your needs and risk tolerance.

Immediate Annuity

As the stock market becomes volatile, more people are looking for an investment that will guarantee an income for a certain period of time, no matter how the investment is performing. Immediate annuities begin to pay you a monthly amount at the time you give the lump sum of money to the insurance company. The insurance company guarantees to pay you a certain percentage of the money each year. It could be for ten years, twenty years, or the rest of your life. The insurance company knows that the fees you will pay them is worth the 'peace of mind' you will have knowing you will never run out of money. **Guaranteed Income for Life** is a very persuasive statement. Before you buy any annuity, *I suggest you speak to a financial professional to review all the pros and cons, costs and riders, which will meet your needs and risk tolerance.*

Deferred Annuity

A deferred annuity is a way to accumulate savings, either through growth or interest, and to take this money sometime in the future. The deferred annuity allows you to defer any tax liability until you begin taking this money. Like other annuities, you can invest in stock or bond mutual funds, or have a fixed interest rate for a fixed period of time. As I stated before, *I suggest you speak to a financial professional to review all the pros and cons, costs and riders, which will meet your needs and risk tolerance.*

As an arbitrator and mediator for FINRA and a consumer advocate on investor education for the past fifteen years, I believe annuities are complex investment products that should be explained, in detail, by a financial professional.

If you have any questions or concerns about your annuity or financial advisor, contact the following agencies:

- National Association of Insurance Commissioners (www.naic.org)
- FINRA (www.finra.org)
- North American Securities Administrators Association (www.nasaa.org)
- National Association of Fixed Annuities (www.nafa.us)

CHAPTER FIVE
LONG TERM CARE INSURANCE

When we talk about investing for retirement, we must also talk about 'what if' situations. Most people only consider an amount of money they will need to cover their normal expenses during retirement. That amount of money becomes meaningless if you or a spouse becomes ill. That is why you must consider long term care insurance.

Long-term care insurance, also known by the initials LTC, helps provide for the out-of-pocket expenses of long-term care not covered by health insurance, Medicare, or Medicaid.

Individuals who require long-term care are generally not considered ill or sick by normal definition. In simple terms, these individuals need help or assistance with the basic activities of daily living. When you think about our daily activities that we take for granted, such as getting out of bed in the morning, going into the bathroom, getting dressed, eating meals, walking from one room to another, LTC insurance is used to help people maintain these daily activities.

Selecting a long term care policy

A long term care insurance policy should be part of your retirement planning for one basic reason: it may protect part to all of your assets. If you decide to purchase LTC, it is important to make sure you select the policy that fits your needs and requirements.

The National Association of Insurance Commissioners (www.naic.org) is a good place to begin your education on selecting the right benefits. Here are some of the benefits they suggest you consider:

* a minimum of one year of nursing home or home health care coverage. * A simple outline of your coverage that describes the policy's benefits, limitations and exclusions.
* Coverage for Alzheimer's disease.
* A policy that protects you against inflation.
* A guarantee that the policy cannot be cancelled because of your health. These are just a few of the questions you should ask.

As with any other decision about an investment, investigate the person and the company selling the plan, and always compare a few companies.

CHAPTER SIX
HOW IMPORTANT
IS THE ACCOUNT FORM?

When you go to a brokerage firm to invest your money, you go with the understanding that the information your broker will provide is accurate and truthful, so that you can make an informed decision on your investments.

Usually, the first time you hear about an investment is either in your advisor's office or on the phone with your advisor. Since he is the professional on investments you accept his advice. You also assume that what he is doing is in your best interest.

A problem can arise months or sometimes years later when you realize that you were sold an investment that you were unsuited for, or an investment about which you did not understand the risks involved.

If this happens to you, and you and the brokerage firm cannot come to an amicable solution, then arbitration or mediation could be your legal remedy.

The arbitration / mediation may take place years after the original conversation between you and your advisor regarding the investment you purchased. I can almost guarantee you that the advisor will remember the conversation differently than you do, thereby making the verbal discussions unreliable and meaningless. That is why the Account Form, usually the only written document the stockbroker has that describes you, becomes so vital in your defense at arbitration.

Thus, the most important and least understood document the stockbroker has a client fill out is the Client Account Form. Every person must fill out an Account Form to receive an account number. This is mandatory before a transaction between you and your broker can occur.

The Client Account Form might look like a basic questionnaire with simple questions, but it is the document that shows if you are suited for certain types of investments. Do not answer these questions lightly or inaccurately. It could cost you dearly in the future.

Before I review the Account Form line by line, I want to emphasize the best advice I can give you. **DON'T EXAGGERATE YOUR EXPERIENCE OR INCOME ON THE ACCOUNT FORM.** If you make $30.000.00 a year, do not state anything higher. When the question is about your investment experience in stocks, bonds, commodities, etc., only put the actual number of years you have been an investor. If you are trying to impress the advisor, **DON'T!** Now I will show you how a brokerage firm could interpret your answers on an Account Form. A standard Client Account Form will contain the following questions:

1. **General Information** - name, address, birth date, social security number, telephone number. *So far no problem.*

2. **Residence** - rent or own. This shows the brokerage firm, right away, that if you own a home, you are not ignorant of all types of investments. Also, if you own a real estate limited partnership you would have some idea of the liquidity and economic risks involved in owning real estate. Thus, if the partnership had decreased in value, you could not claim that you were unaware of the risks in real estate.

3 **Legal residence if different from mailing address** - This shows the brokerage firm if you have more than one home, which is an indication of your assets.

4. **Employment/Job Title/Occupation -** This may show the type of knowledge you might have pertaining to investments in certain industries.

5. **Client state annual income. Client state net worth exclusive of family residence. and estimated liquid net worth - DO NOT EXAGGERATE**. This shows the brokerage firm what portion of your assets is in a specific investment. Having a diversified port folio of no more than 2-5% of total assets in one investment may not be worth as much in an arbitration decision as 50% in one investment.

6. **Is the client on a fixed income - Yes or No -** If you are, then say it. By checking this box the broker should be aware that you have no additional income other than your investments, pensions, and/or social security and that you will probably be a conservative investor.

7. **Is the client an officer, director or 10% stockholder in any corporation** - This tells the brokerage firm that you probably have knowledge about business and investments and also that you have additional assets.

8. **Citizen of U.S.A. (if other please specify)** - If you are not a citizen of the U.S., there may be different tax liabilities depending on your investments and the country that you are from. The stock broker must be aware of this: otherwise, the brokerage firm, not you, could be liable for any losses incurred.

9. **Former client or account with other brokerage firm** - This shows the brokerage firm the type of investments that you may have made in the past. This will also indicate if you are knowledgeable or suited for certain types of investments.

10. **Investment profile** - Very important! If you want safety of principal and income, DON'T SAY GROWTH! Put down only what you want. Also remember, do not put down more investment experience in stock, bonds, options, etc. than what you actually have.

11. **Introduction** - This is where the brokerage firm finds out how you came to open an account. The options are usually seminars, walk/phone in, advertising, personal acquaintance, and referrals. Seminars, personal acquaintances, and referrals may sound innocent, but let me show you what they imply: If you went to a seminar it shows you go out of your way to get knowledge on specific investments. Brokerage firms may say if you have gone to one seminar you may have gone to many and that you are aware of different types of investments and are probably suited for many investments. If you are referred by a person who is knowledgeable about investments, then there is a good chance you have had dis cussions about investments, which could imply that you know more about investments than what is stated on the account form. These are possibilities of how a brokerage firm may look at your account form.

12. **References** - name of bank, If you ever have a problem with the brokerage firm they may want to know about your knowledge of investments, References would be a good place to find out this type of information,

13. **Power of attorney** - This means someone besides yourself has the right to handle the money in your account, as well as decide what investments should be made. Be very careful with this, giving someone else this authority may affect your financial situation forever.

14. **Account description** - cash or margin. Cash accounts are the most common. In a cash account, you buy or sell a security (stock, bond, mutual fund, etc.) and pay or receive 100% of the amount, usually within five business days. A Margin Account gives you the right to borrow money on your account (a loan) by using the securities in the account as collateral. For example: If you buy 200 shares of General Electric at $16.00 a share; the total amount you would owe is $3,200.00. In a Margin Account you could borrow up to 50% of the amount owed, which means you would pay $1,600.00 and the brokerage firm would lend you the other $1,600.00 for as long as you keep the General Electric stock in your account. Like any other loan you will pay interest charges to the brokerage firm for as long as you owe them the $1,600.00. Buying on margin is O.K. **as long as your advisor explains, AND YOU UNDERSTAND,** both the risks and the benefits. It is very important to update the account form if your situation changes, i.e. a spouse dies, your financial situation changes, you retire, etc. Make sure your stockbroker is notified in writing and a new account form is filled out. In case a dispute arises between you and your broker, another fact that you should know is that the stockbroker must be licensed in the state where you are a permanent resident. If you buy securities from an advisor and you lose money, make sure that he was licensed in your state at the time of the transaction. If not, the trade should be voided and you should get all your money back.

CHAPTER SEVEN
WHAT YOU SHOULD KNOW
THAT COULD SAVE YOU MONEY

1. Tell your broker to send you an old copy of the Standard and Poors (S & P) book. This monthly book gives you the name of issue, ticker symbol, rating, principle business, price range, dividend, yield, price earnings ratio, financial position, capitalization, annual earnings, plus information on over 700 mutual funds every month. Most brokers, after a month or two, throw out their old copies. Most of the information does not change so it is a wealth of information that usually ends up in the waste basket. If you were to pay for a subscription to S & P for a year, you would pay $250.00. So, call your broker and save.

SAVINGS: $250.00

2. If you are in the market for mutual funds and are willing to put in the time and effort, use Morningstar or other sources for your research.
   Possible savings: hundreds to thousands of dollars

3. If you decide to buy mutual funds or unit trusts from your broker, make sure he tells you about BREAKPOINTS.

SAVINGS: hundred to thousands of dollars.

4. If you open a margin account at a brokerage firm you should understand what you have at risk. What you are actually doing is taking out a loan and using the securities in your account as collateral, The margin rates charged are usually 1/2% -2 1/2% over the broker loan rate. **MARGIN RATES CAN USUALLY BE NEGOTIATED.** You can usually negotiate savings of 1/2% - 1% on the rate.
   SAVINGS: If you margin $25,000.00, you could save $125.00 - $250.00 per year.

5. There are some mutual funds that charge a sales charge on reinvested income. This means that if you reinvest your income

by buying more shares in the mutual fund, the fund will charge you an additional sales charge to reinvest. So, if you want to reinvest your income, make sure the fund you decide to buy does not have a sales charge to reinvest.

SAVINGS: percentage of all reinvested income.

6. If your advisor sells you a mutual fund and it **does not perform,** or your investment strategy changes, and your advisor tells you to sell the fund and go into another fund, **BEWARE!** Buying a new fund may cost you additional sales charges. Note, however, that exchanging a fund within the same family of funds may cost you very little. Another fund within the same family may meet your investment needs, and to exchange from one fund to another, within the same family, usually has no sales charge or a small administrative fee (five to ten dollars), **DON'T SELL IF YOU CAN EXCHANGE. SAVINGS: Hundreds to thousands of dollars.**

7. Make sure every question on the account form is answered accurately. Most people do not answer all the questions, and this could be harmful because it is a document that could help you in the future. For example, if you state on the account form that what you want is steady income and safety of principal, and on the recommendation of your broker, you purchase stock which does not suit you, then the account form can be used to illustrate your investment goals. Your broker should have realized from the account form that you may have been unsuited for that particular type of investment.

SAVINGS: A lot of aggravation and possibly money.

8. **BEWARE!** Many advisors may suggest what is known as a proprietary product. This could be a mutual fund, or other product, that is sold by the brokerage firm, as well as managed by the brokerage firm itself. Such products enable the firm to make both a commission from selling it, and a continuing fee from managing it. As a result, the firm gives the broker an incentive to sell these products rather than other products. The incentive may be in the form of higher

payouts of commission or special gifts if they sell a certain amount. Before you buy any proprietary product, ask your broker to show you its track record (performance record) for the past one, three, five, and ten years, if possible. You should then compare it to other investments in the same category, and this way you can judge if the recommendation is truly in your best interest.

9.	Clients often ask if the sales load charged when they bought a mutual fund is tax deductible as an expense. The answer is that it usually is not, but there is a strategy. What you can do is to buy a fund in a family of funds which allows switching from one fund to another. Switching is actually a buy and a sell. If you invest $10,000.00 in a fund with a six percent sales load, the net asset value (N.A.V.) is actually only $9,400.00. If you wait a month and then switch to the fund you actually want, you will switch at N.A.V., which, depending on the N.A.V. at that time could give you a short term loss. Because the government changes the tax laws so often, you should call your accountant to see if this is still possible; if it is, you may be able to save a lot of money.

10.	The best way to save money is to know exactly what you need to do to achieve financial freedom. The way to do this is to have a professional financial analysis. A financial analysis is an examination or review of all your assets and liabilities. This review, usually done by a financial professional, includes all your incomes, investments, homes, mortgages, insurance, credit cards, loans, etc. A good financial analysis will give you a "Game Plan" on how to attain your financial goal. Many companies offer financial analysis. A financial analysis will cost between a few hundred dollars to as high as a few thousand dollars. There are financial services companies that offer you a complimentary financial analysis when you become a client of that firm. I strongly recommend every person who is investing for their retirement do a financial analysis.

CHAPTER EIGHT

Life Insurance

Insurance, in simple terms, is a contract between a policy owner, either a person or company, and an insurance company. The insurance company tells the policy owner that, in exchange for money (premiums), the policy owner will transfer the financial risk and burden from themselves to the insurance company. The insurance company gives the policy owner guarantees that under the terms of the contract (policy), if certain conditions are met, the insurance company will fulfill their obligations to the policy owner.

When you talk about insurance, there are many categories. In this chapter I'm going to review only one category: life insurance. I will discuss the different types, and how and why it is used as financial protection and as a source of income for your retirement.

Life insurance simply states that upon the insured individual's death or other event, such as terminal illness, the insurer will pay the beneficiaries a lump sum dollar amount. The insurer may offer the beneficiaries a payout option, based on the terms in the contract.

Under the category of life insurance, there are different sub categories. I will review term insurance, permanent insurance, and universal life insurance.

Term Life Insurance
Term insurance is temporary insurance. It simply means the policy owner pays premiums for a specific period of time. It usually is between one year and thirty years. At the end of that specific period of time the policy owner stops paying the premium and the life insurance company has no more obligation to pay if the insured dies. When the insured is

young, it is usually the least expensive life insurance; but as the insured gets older, the premiums will increase over time.

The downside of term insurance is that when the term ends, and, you want to renew or repurchase insurance, the premiums will be higher. In addition, your health may not be the same as when you purchased the original term insurance. If you now have a medical condition the insurer may increase the premiums or, even worse, may not insure you at all.

Term insurance is usually purchased for a specific, yet temporary, purpose. It is typically purchased by the main income producer of a family that, in case of their death, the mortgage on their house is paid; or the surviving spouse can raise children without the financial burden.

To qualify for term insurance, or permanent insurance, you must meet the insurance company's requirements. These requirements increases and become more detailed as the face amount of the insurance policy increases. As an example, when you fill out the application for life insurance and you are young and in good health, the insurance company might not require any medical or personal history.

Permanent Life Insurance

Since term insurance is for a specific and limited time period, permanent insurance is, as the word implies, permanent. This means that as long as the policy holder pays the premiums, the insurance coverage cannot be cancelled by the insurance company. There are many benefits in purchasing permanent insurance compared to term insurance:

1. The premiums are fixed. They cannot increase as long as the policy owner pays the premium. The first year's premium is the same as the twentieth year premium.
2. The premium payment for permanent insurance is used not only for the payment of the insurance, but also to build up cash value

in the policy. Every year you pay the premiums the cash value increases. There is no cash value in term insurance.

3. The policy owner ALWAYS has access to the cash value. If the owner needs money and requests the insurance company to give them the cash value, the insurance company is required to give the owner the cash value in the policy.

4. The cash value is considered a loan to the policy owner; therefore there is no tax on any gains or appreciation in the cash value.

5. Paying back the loan is 'optional'. If the insured dies and there is still an outstanding balance on the loan, the loan will be deducted from the face value of the insurance policy.

6. Another major benefit of cash value in life insurance is, in many states, the cash value is protected from creditors and is judgment proof.

7. If you forget to pay the premium, you can set it up that the money in the cash value will pay the premium. This way the policy will not lapse for non payment of premium.

Universal Life Insurance

Universal life insurance is permanent insurance, but it gives the policy owner the flexibility on the amount of monthly premium required to maintain the policy. The policy owner of a universal life policy will have a minimum amount and a maximum amount that can be paid to maintain the policy. In permanent whole life insurance the premiums are fixed.

As in any permanent life insurance policy a portion of the premiums pays for the insurance expense, with the other portion of the premium used to fund the 'cash value' of the policy. It is the same in the universal life policy with the exception that the cash value will vary, depending on the amount of premium you pay.

There are several types of universal life insurance policies. They are:

- Fixed universal life insurance,
- Variable universal life insurance,
- Equity indexed universal life insurance.

Each of these universal life policies have different risks associated with the face value and cash value of the policy.

To understand the pros and cons of each type, since they should be considered in planning your retirement and wealth transfer, *I recommend speaking to a financial professional who is knowledgeable in life insurance.*

CHAPTER NINE
FREQUENT QUESTIONS FROM INVESTORS

Over the past seventeen years, I have been a financial author and columnist. I have written many columns and articles for newspapers and magazines on resolving investment disputes, securities arbitration, and the rights of the investor. I have received many questions from concerned investors. Below are questions and answers from past columns. Where applicable, I have included actual arbitration awards that relate to the questions. The arbitration cases may be old, but the same problems and concerns for clients remain today:

QUESTION

I get calls from many brokers wanting my business. They all promise me top service and good value. One particular broker said he worked for a major national firm and was a bond specialist, and said he was trained and totally competent to handle high net worth individuals. Can I believe that if a person works for a national firm that he's trained and competent in what he's doing?

ANSWER

When I worked for Dean Witter in 1984, the training program for brokers was three months preparing for the series seven license, followed by learning the different products the firm sold. Today the industry has become so competitive and costly they want the broker to start cold calling for prospective clients as soon as possible. Time and experience and learning from other brokers helps the broker become competent. There is no assurance that a broker working for a major brokerage firm is competent or honest in the information he is giving. Case in point F.B. against Brokerage Firm and broker. Arbitrators awarded claimant not only compensatory damages but also punitive damages relating to the brokers conduct with claimants account. Arbitrators believed the broker was not competent for the following reasons:

1-   Broker testified that in her opinion, margin did not increase risk.
2-   Broker testified repeatedly that she felt that an investment opera

tion was profitable if it resulted in net realized gains (irrespective of the fact that there might be unrealized losses).

3- Broker testified that she let losses run (in spite of otherwise active trading) because stocks "always come back".

Arbitrators also felt broker was dishonest and devious for the following reasons:

1 Deliberately checking all investment objective boxes in order to circumvent appropriate supervision.

2 Entering a false S1 million net worth on new account papers at a different firm to create the impression of success for a naive client.

3 Deceptive reporting of account results-annualizing a two month realized gain total and offering it as an account return.

QUESTION

I bought a zero-coupon bond from my broker. When I asked what the commission would be, he told me it wouldn't be more than one percent, which was acceptable. Two weeks later my statement arrived. The amount of money I paid for the bonds was down almost five percent. Interest rates had not moved within the two weeks so I knew it wasn't the price fluctuation of the bonds but the commission. Do I have any recourse if the broker tells me one price yet charges me more.?

ANSWER

Bonds are bought and sold" NET " with a markup-markdown. This means the commission you pay is included in the price of the bonds. There is no way you will know the actual commission being charged. unlike stock and mutual fund transactions. Your problem is your broker probably gave you the price of the commission on the face value of the bonds, not the dollar amount you actually paid. One percent on the face value could be five percent or more on the value of a deep discount bond, like your zero coupon bond. An example, a 100,000.00 bond with $1,000 in commission is one percent. But a 100,000.00 zero coupon bond which matures in twenty five years might cost $20,000.00. Now the $1,000 commission is five percent of your actual cost, which could be an excessive commission.

B.C. against Brokerage Firm

Claimant purchased $60,000.00 face amount stripped zero coupon treasury bonds, maturing in thirty years. Since the price of the bonds was only a fraction of the face value, claimant felt S600.00 commission was excessive. Arbitrators agreed. November,1989, New York.

QUESTION

My broker is recommending I sell the mutual fund I am in and buy another one which is doing better. He told me there would be a sale charge when I buy the new fund. He wants me to sign something called a "switch letter". Can you give me advice on whether I should sign it?

ANSWER

Your broker is following the correct procedure. When switching funds of different families a switch letter states you understand there is a sales charge involved when selling one fund and buying a different fund. It should also state your investment objective is suitable for the new fund. and you are switching because your broker says you were unable to
exchange within your original family of funds to meet your new objectives.

QUESTION

I am a widow age 71 and live off the assets of my husband's estate which are substantial. My broker is the same broker my husband used when he was alive and trusted him implicitly. Two years ago my broker recommended that I give him power of attorney to trade my account. This seemed to make sense since I never understood any of the securities he bought and sold so there was no reason for him to call me before each trade. Even through I don't understand the statements the broker sends me, I can see my net worth has gone down every month over the last year, and my net worth is down over $60,000.00. Was I wrong giving him power of attorney? Should I see a lawyer?

ANSWER

Your broker may not have been worthy of the trust your husband or you put in him. It is seldom necessary for an investor to give a power of attorney to a broker. You should be the ultimate decision maker of your account. If you don't understand all the facts of the transaction your broker is recommending, make an appointment to meet in person and have him explain it to you. If you still can't understand his recommendations, perhaps his strategy is too sophisticated in light of your age and investment objectives. Ask him to give you a brochure or prospectus and take it to another broker or your accountant for their opinion. You may also be able to recover damages for the type of trading he undertook. In the case T.& P.T. against Brokerage Firm and brokers, an arbitration panel awarded the claimant damages for the broker's trading of options and speculative securities pursuant to a power of attorney, December,1989, Florida.

QUESTION

I inherited municipal bonds that my husband had purchased when he passed away. When they matured, we were not able to get as high a rate so the broker said I should go on margin so I could purchase almost three times as many bonds and therefore generate greater income, He said that because the bonds were top quality, I was completely protected. Recently. I got a margin telegram and since I didn't have the money to pay off the margin bill, the brokerage firm liquidated a lot of my bonds. Now My account is worth much less than had I just purchased new bonds at the lower rate. What happened, was I defrauded?

ANSWER

No matter how conservative the investment, once it is purchased on margin it assumes substantially more risk. Margin is when you borrow money from the brokerage firm and use your securities as collateral to buy more securities. One factor which effects the value of the bonds is interest rates. If interest rates go up, the price of your bonds will go down. With quality bonds, you could borrow on margin almost three times the value of the original bonds. which means if the value of your bonds drop $1,000, on margin, your account value could drop $3,000. If the value of the bonds go down to much, the brokerage firm may require more money or they will sell off some of your bonds to cover your margin call. In the arbitration case R.S. against Brokerage Firm, the panel returned an award to the claimant where the failure to advise of the risks of trading bonds on margin was a factor. September, 1990, Florida.

QUESTION

My husband and I intend to retire next year. Two years ago our broker sold my husband some stock his firm underwrote. and guaranteed that them would increase no less than 10% in value within a short period of time. Although we were not looking for quick growth, and questioned whether these stocks were suitable for us, he said we couldn't lose. These issues quickly went down to half of what we paid for them. Can we bring an action against the broker and his firm even through we gave in and let him sell us the stocks?

ANSWER

If these securities were unsuitable for you because of your age, financial situation, and investment objective the broker should not have suggested them to you in the first place. In addition, if you were uncomfortable with his goal of quick growth, he should not have pressured you into the stock. In the NASD arbitration case the panel awarded damages to the claimant and found the broker and the firm liable for the sale of unsuitable equity securities underwritten by the firm. June, 1991, Florida.

QUESTION

When my husband died at age 74, his broker, with whom he had become good friends became my broker. Over the next few years, he not only assisted me with my investment but helped me straighten out my finances and pay my bills, as well as driving me to the doctor's office. Two years ago, he asked me for what I thought was a short-term loan of $50,000.00. He still has not paid back the money and says it was a gift. Can I bring an action to recover my $50,000.00?

ANSWER

Your broker seems to have taken advantage of your vulnerable situation. he should not have asked you to loan him money, not withstanding any assistance he gives you with finances or befriends you in other areas. In L.W.& T.B. against Brokerage Firm and broker, an arbitration panel found the broker liable for selling the claimant unsuitable investments (limited partnerships and option and income funds). and civil theft in connection with his influencing the claimant to issue him checks.

The claimant was awarded treble damages against the broker for the civil theft charge.

QUESTION

I bought a Limited Partnership and some funds from a brokerage firm. Even though the broker gave me a prospectus for the Funds and the Partnerships he did not explain how it's almost impossible to sell the partnership or that there was a big commission in the funds and that it invested in poor quality bonds and options. Because I was given a prospectus and didn't complain right away, does that keep me from bringing an arbitration suit now?

ANSWER

No. Receipt of a prospectus or not filing for arbitration right away does not necessarily bar an investor from getting his money back from a brokerage firm due to an unsuitable investment. In the brokerage industry there is Rule 405 "KNOW YOUR CLIENT", Just because the broker gives you information on the investment doesn't mean your suitable for it. In the case B. & J.G. against Brokerage Firm, claimants who had received a prospectus got back their money based on unsuitable investments and the broker's failure to explain the risks involved in purchasing the investments. Florida, 1989

QUESTION

I know nothing about securities, so I rely on my broker's advice. I am finding however that he is constantly making trades in my account. Most of the buy and sell slips that I receive do not show a commission. Does this mean it does not cost me anything for my broker to make the trades? Since I'm retired, is this the kind of trading okay for my account?

ANSWER

It sounds like there's a possibility of excessive trading, or churning in your account. Just because you do not see your commission as a dollar amount on the confirmation does not mean the broker did not make money on the trade. Brokers should not make trades in your account until they have completely explain the transaction to you and you have given your okay. In the case between HS and GKS&Co. the brokerage firm was found liable for unauthorized trades in the clients account and the monies were returned to the claimant. August,1990, Florida.

QUESTION

Because I am a widow and live on Social Security and the income off my investments, my broker recommended a High Income Fund when my husband passed away in 1988. The fund has subsequently gone up and down. and although it has provided relatively high income. I'm not comfortable seeing the value of my money change all the time. I cannot however get out of the fund and recover my principal anymore. Is there anything I can do?

ANSWER

If your broker omitted the fact that your money could have substantial fluctuation, you may have a cause of action. In a case of where the claimant was a widow seeking" safe" low risk alternatives to CDs. The claimant alleged the broker made misrepresentations of and omitted material facts in the high income government where the claimant suffered a substantial loss of principal. The arbitration panel returned a substantial amount of money to the claimant, Florida,1991.

Last year I sold my house and had $100,000 to invest. I told my broker I wanted income and growth. He recommended I split the money into two mutual funds. He told me what the commissions would be and what yield I would get on my money. I agreed to buy the funds. I now found out I could have saved almost $1,000.00 on the commission if my broker would have put me in the same type of mutual funds in the same family of funds. Is the broker required to tell me about this discount?

ANSWER

The broker has a moral obligation but is not legally required to inform you of this discount, known as breakpoints. Breakpoints are determined by the amount you are investing within a family of funds. A sales charge can be reduced from 51/2% to literally nothing. You should have received a prospectus of these funds telling you the sales charge and breakpoints..

Here is an arbitration case where breakpoints were a factor: In H.F. vs. E.K. Group Securities, H.F alleged respondent failed to inform claimant of price break and letter of intent that he was entitled to. Arbitrators awarded H.F. $1,305. October,1989, Florida

QUESTION

My broker called me about a new mutual fund his firm was selling. He said it would be traded like a stock and would give me a monthly income. What made me interested was that he said I can buy it and not pay any commission. I know my broker has to make commissions to make a living and brokerage firms don't do anything for free, can you explain what this is?

ANSWER

The broker wants to sell you a closed-end bond fund that is having its initial public offering. It is true you are not directly paying the broker's commission. He is paid by the company making the public offering. The problem is the net asset value of each share your purchasing will be less then the price your paying. Remember, closed-end funds have two prices; the market value, which is the price you buy or sell it for; and the net asset value (NAV) which is the actually value of each share. You should also realize you would not receive your first check for 90 days because the fund has to go into the open market to buy the bonds and that takes time. Instead of buying this new fund you might be better off buying a closed end fund that has been out for six months or a year. This way you do not have to wait 90 days for your first payment. Also there probably won't be a large spread between the market value and the NAV.

QUESTION

I've just received my year end statement from my brokerage firm. I brought it to my accountant, which I do every year so he can do my taxes. He made me aware of losses, which I had no idea I had. My broker never told me of these losses or transactions that resulted in these losses. When I called my broker and asked him to explain these trades he told me we discussed each one. That is just not true. What recourse do I have?

ANSWER

The year end statement from your brokerage firm is an excellent summary to review the entire years transactions and values. It's a quick way to find out gains and losses without having to get out each buy and sell confirmation. If you feel there were transactions that were unauthorized by you then you would have recourse against the broker if you can prove they were unauthorized.

W.R. AND B.R, against Merrill Lynch. Claimants alleged Merrill Lynch failed to follow trading instructions, and executed unauthorized trades. Merrill Lynch denied allegation and stated claimant either authorized or ratified all trades. Arbitrators gave award to claimant. February 1990, Florida.

I'm angry. My broker recommended that I buy a high yield bond fund. I did not understand what the risk was. When I found out how risky it was, I sold it and lost S 2,600.00. The broker and his firm say there is nothing they can do. I went to a lawyer and he said there isn't enough money involved for him or probably any lawyer to take his case. What can I do. Please help.

ANSWER

You can do something. First, you do not need a lawyer to file for arbitration. Contact the National Association of Securities Dealers at 212-858-4000 They will send you the information and forms you need to file. Second, the N.A.S.D. has what is called "simplified arbitration" which are for claims for $ 25,000.00 or less. The costs to you are less than an arbitration with a panel of arbitrators. Many cases are filed for simplified arbitration.

One example: J & CF against Kidder Peabody & company. Customer alleges broker failed to follow instructions to sell mutual funds. He filed for $1,280.00 and was awarded $1,025.00. August, 1989. Los Angeles, Ca.

CPSIA information can be obtained at www.ICGtesting.com

225425LV00002B/16/P

9 780962 981166